THE DIGITAL GOLD RUSH

BECOME A MILLIONAIRE IN THE AGE OF DIGITAL MEDIA

Includes Example Strategies

NATHAN SHEWRING

For All The Winners Out There

Contents

Overview

Introduction

The introduction sets the stage by discussing the unprecedented growth of digital media and its potential to create millionaires. It will highlight the importance of understanding digital platforms and leveraging them to build a substantial income.

Chapter 1: The Rise of Digital Media

This chapter will explore the evolution of digital media, from its humble beginnings to its current status as a dominant force in the global economy. Key milestones, such as the advent of social media, streaming services, and the influencer economy, will be covered.

Chapter 2: Identifying Lucrative Opportunities

Readers will learn how to identify profitable niches within the digital media landscape. This includes content creation, digital marketing, e-commerce, and emerging trends like NFTs and the metaverse.

Chapter 3: Building a Personal Brand

A strong personal brand is crucial for success in digital media. This chapter will provide practical advice on creating and maintaining a compelling personal brand, including tips on social media presence, content strategy, and audience engagement.

Chapter 4: Monetisation Strategies

Different monetisation strategies will be explored in depth. This includes ad revenue, sponsored content, affiliate marketing, merchandise sales, subscription models, and crowdfunding. Real-life success stories will illustrate each strategy.

Chapter 5: Leveraging Technology

An overview of essential tools and technologies that can amplify success in digital media. Topics will include SEO, analytics, automation tools, and the use of AI to enhance content creation and distribution.

Chapter 6: Case Studies

Detailed case studies of individuals and businesses that have achieved millionaire status through digital media. These will provide practical insights and inspiration for readers.

Chapter 7: Challenges and Pitfalls

This chapter will discuss the common challenges and pitfalls faced in the digital media industry, such as platform dependency, burnout, and maintaining relevance. Strategies for overcoming these challenges will be provided.

Chapter 8: The Future of Digital Media

A forward-looking perspective on where digital media is headed. Topics might include the impact of new technologies, evolving consumer behaviours, and potential new opportunities.

Chapter 9: Emerging Trends in Digital Media

Explores short-form content, AR/VR's role, AI's impact on personalisation, live streaming benefits, data privacy, platform diversification, and emerging trends in digital media's future.

Chapter 10: Building a Sustainable Digital Media Business

Details how to go about building a sustainable digital media business with long-term strategies, effective branding, audience engagement, and diversified revenue streams.

Conclusion

A recap of the key takeaways and an empowering message to encourage readers to start their journey toward becoming a digital media millionaire.

Appendices

Three example approaches, additional resources, including recommended reading, useful websites, and a glossary of terms.

Introduction

The world is witnessing a revolutionary shift, one that is as significant as the industrial revolution: the rise of digital media. Over the past few decades, the way we communicate, consume content, and do business has transformed dramatically, thanks to the advent of digital technologies. From the proliferation of social media platforms to the explosion of online video content, digital media has become an integral part of our daily lives, influencing how we interact, learn, and entertain ourselves.

But beyond its pervasive presence, digital media represents an unprecedented opportunity for wealth creation. The digital landscape is teeming with possibilities for those willing to innovate, adapt, and leverage its vast potential. Whether you're a content creator, entrepreneur, marketer, or someone with a passion and a vision, the digital world offers numerous avenues to build substantial wealth and even achieve millionaire status.

Consider the stories of individuals like PewDiePie, who turned his passion for gaming into a multi-million-dollar YouTube empire, or Kylie Jenner, who leveraged her social media influence to build a billion-dollar cosmetics brand. These success stories are not outliers; they are indicative of a broader trend where digital media is democratising opportunities, enabling ordinary people to achieve extraordinary financial success.

In this book, "The Digital Gold Rush: How to Become a Millionaire in the Age of Digital Media," we will explore the vast and varied landscape of digital media and uncover the secrets to capitalising on its potential. We will delve into the evolution of digital platforms, examine lucrative opportunities, and provide practical strategies for building a personal brand, monetising content, and leveraging technology.

You will learn from real-life case studies of digital media millionaires, gain insights into overcoming common challenges, and get a glimpse into the future of this dynamic field. Whether you're just starting out or looking to scale your existing efforts, this book aims to equip you with the knowledge and tools to embark on your journey toward digital wealth.

Welcome to the digital gold rush. The tools and opportunities to become a millionaire are at your fingertips. It's time to dig in and stake your claim.

Chapter 1: The Rise of Digital Media

In the span of a few short decades, digital media has transformed from a niche interest into a global phenomenon that shapes every aspect of modern life. This chapter explores the evolution of digital media, tracing its origins, key milestones, and the factors that have contributed to its explosive growth. Understanding this history is crucial for anyone looking to capitalise on the opportunities that digital media presents.

The Early Days: From Static Web to Social Interaction

The internet's early days were marked by static websites and simple email communication. In the mid-1990s, the World Wide Web began to take shape, offering a new way for people to access and share information. Early pioneers like AOL, Yahoo!, and GeoCities provided platforms for users to create and explore content. However, these early experiences were largely one-way streets, with content creators publishing information and users passively consuming it.

The introduction of Web 2.0 in the early 2000s marked a significant turning point. This new era was characterised by increased interactivity, user-generated content, and the rise of social media platforms. Sites like MySpace, Facebook, and YouTube emerged, allowing users to connect, share, and create in ways that were previously unimaginable. This shift democratised content creation, giving rise to the concept of the "prosumer" – individuals who both consume and produce media.

Key Milestones in Digital Media

Several key milestones have shaped the digital media landscape we know today:

1. **The Launch of YouTube (2005)**: YouTube revolutionised video content creation and consumption. It provided a platform for anyone with a camera and an internet connection to share their videos with a global audience. The viral nature of YouTube

content and the introduction of monetisation options allowed creators to turn their hobbies into profitable careers.

2. **The Rise of Social Media (2004-2010)**: Platforms like Facebook, Twitter, and Instagram changed the way people interact online. They provided new channels for communication, marketing, and brand building. The power of social media influencers began to grow, as individuals with large followings could sway opinions and drive trends.

3. **The Smartphone Revolution (2007)**: The introduction of the iPhone and the subsequent proliferation of smartphones put the internet in everyone's pocket. This accessibility fuelled the growth of mobile apps, social media usage, and on-the-go content consumption, further embedding digital media into everyday life.

4. **The Advent of Streaming Services (2010s)**: Services like Netflix, Spotify, and Twitch changed how we consume entertainment. Streaming offered convenience, variety, and personalisation, challenging traditional media formats like television and radio. Content creators could now reach audiences directly, bypassing traditional gatekeepers.

5. **The Emergence of Influencer Marketing (2010s)**: As social media platforms grew, so did the influence of individuals who amassed large followings. Brands began to recognise the value of partnering with these influencers to reach targeted audiences authentically. This new marketing paradigm shifted significant advertising dollars from traditional media to digital platforms.

The Driving Forces Behind Digital Media Growth

Several factors have contributed to the rapid growth and dominance of digital media:

1. **Technological Advancements**: Innovations in technology, including faster internet speeds, improved mobile devices, and sophisticated algorithms, have made digital media more accessible and engaging. These advancements have lowered barriers to entry, enabling more people to create and consume content.

2. **Changing Consumer Behaviours**: Today's consumers expect instant access to information and entertainment. They value convenience, personalisation, and interactivity, all of which digital media provides in abundance. This shift in preferences has driven the adoption of digital platforms over traditional media.

3. **Economic Opportunities**: The digital media ecosystem offers numerous monetisation opportunities. From ad revenue and sponsored content to e-commerce and subscription models, creators and businesses can generate significant income through various digital channels. This potential for financial reward has attracted a diverse array of participants to the digital media landscape.

4. **Global Connectivity**: The internet has made the world more interconnected than ever before. Digital media transcends geographic boundaries, allowing creators to reach global audiences. This interconnectedness fosters cultural exchange, broadens perspectives, and creates opportunities for cross-border collaborations.

Chapter Conclusion

The rise of digital media is a testament to the transformative power of technology and innovation. From its early beginnings to its current status as a dominant force in the global economy, digital media has revolutionised how we communicate, consume content, and do business. By understanding the history and key drivers of digital media growth, you can better navigate this dynamic landscape and seize the opportunities it presents.

In the following chapters, we will delve deeper into specific strategies and insights that can help you become a digital media millionaire. Whether you're a content creator, entrepreneur, or marketer, the digital gold rush offers endless possibilities for those willing to explore, experiment, and evolve.

Chapter 2: Identifying Lucrative Opportunities

The digital media landscape is vast and diverse, offering a plethora of opportunities for those looking to build wealth. However, identifying the most lucrative niches and understanding how to capitalise on them is essential for success. In this chapter, we will explore various segments within digital media that present significant earning potential. From content creation and digital marketing to e-commerce and emerging trends, we will uncover the pathways to financial success in the digital age.

Content Creation: The Heart of Digital Media

Content is king in the digital world, and content creation remains one of the most promising avenues for generating income. Here are some key areas within content creation:

1. **Video Content**: Platforms like YouTube, TikTok, and Twitch have turned ordinary individuals into internet celebrities. By creating engaging, high-quality videos, content creators can attract large audiences and monetise their channels through ad revenue, sponsorships, and merchandise sales. Successful niches include gaming, beauty, lifestyle, education, and comedy.
2. **Blogging and Writing**: While video content dominates, written content remains a valuable asset. Bloggers and freelance writers can earn money through advertising, sponsored posts, affiliate marketing, and subscription-based models. Niches such as personal finance, health and wellness, travel, and technology are particularly profitable.
3. **Podcasting**: The resurgence of audio content has led to a boom in podcasting. Podcasters can monetise their shows through sponsorships, listener donations, and premium content offerings. Topics range from true crime and self-improvement to business and entertainment, allowing for a wide range of interests to be catered to.

4. **Social Media Influencing**: Social media influencers leverage their large followings on platforms like Instagram, Twitter, and Facebook to partner with brands and promote products. Influencers can earn significant income through sponsored posts, affiliate marketing, and brand ambassadorships. Micro-influencers, with smaller but highly engaged audiences, are also finding lucrative opportunities.

Digital Marketing: The Backbone of Online Success

Digital marketing is essential for driving traffic, engagement, and sales in the digital age. Here are some profitable areas within digital marketing:

1. **SEO and Content Marketing**: Search Engine Optimisation (SEO) and content marketing help businesses improve their online visibility and attract organic traffic. Experts in this field can offer consulting services, create SEO-optimised content, and manage comprehensive content strategies for clients.
2. **Social Media Management**: Businesses of all sizes need a strong social media presence. Social media managers create, schedule, and analyse content to build brand awareness and drive engagement. Offering social media management services can be highly profitable, especially for those who stay up to date with platform algorithms and trends.
3. **Email Marketing**: Despite the rise of social media, email marketing remains one of the most effective digital marketing strategies. Professionals in this field design email campaigns, manage subscriber lists, and analyse campaign performance to maximise ROI. Creating and selling email marketing templates or courses can also be lucrative.
4. **Pay-Per-Click (PPC) Advertising**: PPC specialists manage online advertising campaigns on platforms like Google Ads and Facebook Ads. By optimising ad spend and targeting the right audiences, they help businesses achieve their marketing goals. Offering PPC services or training can be a substantial income source.

E-commerce: The Digital Marketplace

E-commerce has revolutionised retail, providing endless opportunities for entrepreneurs. Here are some profitable e-commerce models:

1. **Dropshipping**: Dropshipping allows entrepreneurs to sell products without holding inventory. By partnering with suppliers, they can create online stores and fulfil orders directly through the suppliers. This low-risk model has become popular due to its minimal upfront investment.
2. **Print on Demand**: Print on demand enables entrepreneurs to sell custom-designed products like t-shirts, mugs, and phone cases without holding inventory. When a customer places an order, the product is printed and shipped by a third-party provider. This model is ideal for creatives looking to monetise their designs.
3. **Private Labelling**: Private labelling involves sourcing generic products from manufacturers and branding them with your own label. This model allows for greater control over product quality and branding. Entrepreneurs can sell private label products on platforms like Amazon or their own e-commerce sites.
4. **Subscription Boxes**: Subscription box services deliver curated products to customers on a recurring basis. This model creates a steady revenue stream and builds customer loyalty. Popular niches include beauty, fitness, food, and hobbies.

Emerging Trends: The Future of Digital Media

Staying ahead of emerging trends is crucial for long-term success in digital media. Here are some cutting-edge opportunities:

1. **NFTs and Digital Art**: Non-fungible tokens (NFTs) have revolutionised the art world by allowing digital artists to sell their work directly to collectors. NFTs can represent anything from digital art and music to virtual real estate and collectibles. Creators can earn substantial income by minting and selling NFTs on platforms like OpenSea and Rarible.

2. **The Metaverse**: The metaverse is an immersive virtual world where people can interact, work, and play. As the metaverse expands, opportunities for creating and selling virtual goods, services, and experiences will grow. Entrepreneurs can develop virtual real estate, create virtual fashion, or offer metaverse-based events and entertainment.
3. **Online Courses and E-Learning**: The demand for online education continues to rise. Experts in various fields can create and sell online courses, e-books, and webinars. Platforms like Udemy, Teachable, and Coursera provide the infrastructure to reach global audiences and generate passive income.
4. **Health and Wellness Tech**: The intersection of technology and health is creating new opportunities for digital entrepreneurs. From fitness apps and wearable devices to telehealth services and mental health platforms, the health and wellness tech industry is poised for significant growth.

How to Discover Your Niche

Choosing the right niche is a critical step in building a successful digital media presence, whether it's a YouTube channel, blog, or podcast. Your niche defines the specific topic or audience focus of your content, and it will guide your content strategy, branding, and marketing efforts. Here's a step-by-step guide to discovering your niche:

1. Self-Assessment:

- **Passion and Interest:** Start by identifying topics you are passionate about. What are the subjects you can talk about endlessly without getting bored? Your enthusiasm will translate into engaging content and sustained motivation.
- **Expertise and Knowledge:** Consider areas where you have substantial knowledge or expertise. What subjects do people come to you for advice on? Your unique insights and skills can set you apart in your chosen niche.
- **Experience and Background:** Reflect on your personal and professional experiences. How can you leverage your

background to provide valuable content? Your unique perspective can add depth to your niche.

2. Market Research:

- **Identify Trends:** Use tools like Google Trends, social media platforms, and industry reports to identify trending topics and emerging interests. Understanding what's currently popular can help you align your niche with audience demand.
- **Analyse Competitors:** Look at successful creators or influencers in potential niches. What are they doing well? Where are the gaps in their content? Analysing competitors can provide insights into what works and what opportunities exist.
- **Audience Analysis:** Use audience insights tools available on platforms like YouTube, Instagram, or podcast analytics to understand what content resonates with viewers or listeners. Demographic information, viewing habits, and engagement metrics can guide your niche selection.

3. Evaluate Niche Viability:

- **Audience Size:** Assess the potential size of your target audience. A niche that's too broad may dilute your content, while one that's too narrow may limit your audience reach. Look for a balance between specificity and reach.
- **Monetisation Potential:** Consider the monetisation opportunities within your niche. Are there brands willing to sponsor content? Is there demand for products or services related to the niche? Evaluate the commercial viability of your chosen topic.
- **Longevity and Sustainability:** Ensure your niche has long-term potential. Avoid fads or highly seasonal topics unless you have a strategy for maintaining relevance. Sustainable niches offer consistent opportunities for content creation and growth.

4. Test and Iterate:

- **Content Experiments:** Create a few pieces of content on different topics within your potential niche. Monitor the response and engagement from your audience. Use this feedback to refine your focus.
- **Engage with Your Audience:** Ask your audience directly for their interests and preferences. Conduct surveys, polls, or Q&A sessions to gather insights. Audience feedback can validate your niche choice and help tailor your content strategy.
- **Analyse Performance:** Use analytics tools to track the performance of your test content. Pay attention to metrics like views, likes, comments, shares, and retention rates. These metrics can indicate which topics resonate most with your audience.

5. Commit to Your Niche:

- **Create a Content Plan:** Once you've identified a viable niche, develop a comprehensive content plan. Outline your content types, posting schedule, and key themes. Consistent planning ensures a steady stream of content and keeps your audience engaged.
- **Branding and Positioning:** Develop a strong brand identity that aligns with your niche. This includes your name, logo, colour scheme, and overall aesthetic. Clear branding helps establish your presence and attract your target audience.
- **Engage and Grow:** Focus on building a community around your niche. Engage with your audience regularly through comments, social media interactions, and email newsletters. A dedicated community will support your growth and amplify your reach.

By following these steps, you can discover a niche that aligns with your passions, leverages your expertise, and meets market demand. A well-chosen niche sets the foundation for a successful digital media presence, enabling you to create compelling content, attract a loyal audience, and achieve your goals.

Chapter Conclusion

The digital media landscape offers a wealth of opportunities for those willing to explore and innovate. Whether you're drawn to content creation, digital marketing, e-commerce, or emerging trends, there's a path to financial success waiting for you. By identifying lucrative niches and leveraging the power of digital platforms, you can turn your passion and expertise into a thriving business.

In the following chapters, we will dive deeper into specific strategies for building a personal brand, monetising your efforts, and overcoming challenges. The digital gold rush is here, and with the right knowledge and determination, you can stake your claim and achieve millionaire status in the age of digital media.

Chapter 3: Building a Personal Brand

In the digital age, building a strong personal brand is crucial for success. Your personal brand is how you present yourself to the world and how others perceive you. It's a combination of your online presence, reputation, and the value you offer to your audience. This chapter will guide you through the steps to create and maintain a compelling personal brand that can help you stand out in a crowded digital landscape and attract lucrative opportunities.

Understanding the Importance of Personal Branding

A personal brand is more than just a logo or a catchy tagline. It is a reflection of your values, skills, personality, and the unique perspective you bring to your field. A strong personal brand can:

1. **Differentiate You from the Competition**: In a saturated market, your personal brand sets you apart from others. It highlights what makes you unique and why people should follow, hire, or buy from you.

2. **Build Trust and Credibility**: Consistently sharing valuable content and engaging with your audience establishes you as an authority in your niche. Trust and credibility are essential for attracting opportunities and loyal followers.

3. **Attract Opportunities**: A well-crafted personal brand can open doors to speaking engagements, partnerships, sponsorships, and other opportunities. Brands and businesses are more likely to collaborate with individuals who have a strong, positive online presence.

4. **Increase Your Earning Potential**: A recognisable personal brand can lead to higher-paying opportunities, whether you're a freelancer, consultant, content creator, or entrepreneur. People are willing to pay a premium for expertise and reliability.

Steps to Building Your Personal Brand

1. **Define Your Brand Identity**

   o **Identify Your Unique Selling Proposition (USP):** What
      sets you apart from others in your field? What unique
      skills, experiences, or perspectives do you bring? Your
      USP is the foundation of your personal brand.

   o **Clarify Your Values and Mission:** What do you stand
      for? What are your core values and goals? Your brand
      should reflect what you believe in and aim to achieve.

   o **Understand Your Target Audience:** Who are you trying
      to reach? Knowing your audience's needs, interests, and
      pain points will help you create content and engage in
      ways that resonate with them.

2. **Create a Cohesive Visual Identity**

   o **Design a Professional Logo:** A logo is a visual
      representation of your brand. It should be simple,
      memorable, and reflective of your brand identity.

   o **Choose a Consistent Colour Scheme and Typography:**
      Consistency in visual elements helps in creating a
      recognisable brand. Use the same colours and fonts
      across all your platforms.

   o **Develop a Professional Website:** Your website is your
      digital home base. It should be well-designed, easy to
      navigate, and include essential information about you,
      your services, and how to contact you.

3. **Build Your Online Presence**

   o **Social Media Profiles**: Create and optimise profiles on relevant social media platforms like LinkedIn, Twitter, Instagram, Facebook, and YouTube. Use the same handle, profile picture, and bio across platforms for consistency.

   o **Content Creation**: Share valuable content that showcases your expertise and provides value to your audience. This can include blog posts, videos, podcasts, infographics, and social media updates.

   o **Engage with Your Audience**: Respond to comments, participate in discussions, and engage with other influencers in your niche. Building relationships and a sense of community is key to growing your following.

4. **Showcase Your Expertise**

   o **Create High-Quality Content**: Focus on creating content that is informative, entertaining, and relevant to your audience. Quality content establishes you as an authority in your field.

   o **Guest Blogging and Podcasting**: Write guest posts for popular blogs in your niche or appear as a guest on podcasts. This expands your reach and introduces you to new audiences.

   o **Public Speaking and Workshops**: Speaking at events, hosting webinars, or conducting workshops can further establish your credibility and attract more followers.

5. **Network and Collaborate**

   o **Join Professional Organisations and Online Communities**: Being part of industry groups and forums allows you to network with like-minded individuals and stay updated on industry trends.

   o **Collaborate with Influencers and Brands**: Partnering with other influencers or brands can help you reach new audiences and build your credibility. Look for collaboration opportunities that align with your brand values.

6. **Monitor and Adapt**

   o **Track Your Performance**: Use analytics tools to monitor your social media performance, website traffic, and content engagement. Understanding what works and what doesn't will help you refine your strategy.

   o **Stay Updated on Trends**: The digital landscape is constantly evolving. Stay informed about new platforms, tools, and trends in your industry to keep your brand relevant.

   o **Adapt and Evolve**: Be flexible and willing to adapt your brand strategy as needed. Growth and change are part of building a successful personal brand.

Case Studies of Successful Personal Brands

1. **Gary Vaynerchuk**: Gary Vaynerchuk, also known as GaryVee, built his personal brand by sharing his expertise in entrepreneurship, social media, and digital marketing. He consistently produces high-quality content across multiple platforms and engages with his audience regularly. His

authenticity and no-nonsense advice have garnered a massive following and numerous business opportunities.

2. **Marie Forleo**: Marie Forleo is a life coach, author, and motivational speaker. She created her brand around empowering others to create a life and business they love. Through her popular online show "MarieTV" and best-selling books, she provides valuable advice and inspiration to her audience. Her consistent branding and positive message have made her a trusted authority in the self-help industry.

3. **Neil Patel**: Neil Patel is a digital marketing expert known for his in-depth content on SEO, content marketing, and digital strategy. By consistently publishing high-quality articles, videos, and podcasts, he has established himself as a leading voice in the digital marketing space. His personal brand has attracted numerous speaking engagements, consulting opportunities, and a loyal following.

Chapter Conclusion

Building a personal brand is a journey that requires time, effort, and consistency. By defining your brand identity, creating a cohesive visual presence, and engaging with your audience through valuable content, you can establish yourself as a trusted authority in your field. Networking, collaboration, and staying adaptable to industry trends will further enhance your brand and open up lucrative opportunities.

In the next chapter, we will explore various monetisation strategies that can help you turn your personal brand into a thriving business. The digital gold rush is not just about creating content but also about smartly monetising your efforts to achieve financial success.

Chapter 4: Monetisation Strategies

Once you've established a strong personal brand and built a loyal audience, the next step is to monetise your efforts. There are numerous strategies to generate income through digital media, each with its own benefits and challenges. This chapter will explore various monetisation methods, providing insights and real-life examples to help you determine the best approach for your brand.

1. Advertising Revenue

Advertising is one of the most common ways to monetise digital content. Here are some key advertising revenue streams:

A. Display Ads

Display ads are banner ads that appear on your website or blog. You can join ad networks like Google AdSense, Media.net, or Ezoic, which automatically place relevant ads on your site. You earn money based on the number of impressions or clicks these ads receive.

Example: A popular lifestyle blog that attracts thousands of daily visitors can generate substantial income through display ads. The key is to create high-quality content that attracts a large and engaged audience.

B. Video Ads

If you're a video content creator on platforms like YouTube, you can earn money through video ads. YouTube's Partner Program allows you to monetise your videos with ads, and you earn revenue based on ad views and clicks.

Example: PewDiePie, one of the most popular YouTubers, generates significant income from video ads due to his massive subscriber base and high video view counts.

C. Sponsored Content and Brand Deals

Sponsored content involves partnering with brands to create content that promotes their products or services. Brands pay you to create blog posts, videos, or social media posts featuring their offerings.

Example: Fashion and beauty influencers often collaborate with brands to create sponsored Instagram posts or YouTube videos showcasing products. These collaborations can be highly lucrative, especially for influencers with large followings.

2. Affiliate Marketing

Affiliate marketing involves promoting products or services and earning a commission for each sale made through your referral link. This method is popular among bloggers, YouTubers, and social media influencers.

Steps to Get Started:

- Join affiliate programs or networks like Amazon Associates, ShareASale, or Commission Junction.

- Select products or services that align with your brand and audience.

- Create content that naturally incorporates your affiliate links, such as product reviews, tutorials, or recommendations.

Example: A tech blogger might write detailed reviews of gadgets and include affiliate links to purchase those products. Each time a reader buys through those links, the blogger earns a commission.

3. Selling Digital Products

Creating and selling digital products is a scalable way to monetise your expertise. Digital products have low overhead costs and can be sold repeatedly without additional effort.

A. E-books and Guides

Write and sell e-books or guides that provide valuable information to your audience. Platforms like Amazon Kindle Direct Publishing (KDP) make it easy to self-publish and distribute your work.

Example: A fitness influencer might create an e-book with workout plans and nutritional advice. Selling this e-book to their followers provides a steady stream of income.

B. Online Courses and Workshops

Online courses and workshops allow you to share your knowledge in a structured format. Platforms like Udemy, Teachable, and Coursera enable you to create and sell courses on various topics.

Example: An experienced marketer might create an online course on digital marketing strategies. By promoting the course to their audience, they can generate significant revenue.

C. Printables and Templates

Design and sell digital products like printables, templates, or planners. These products are easy to create and can be sold on platforms like Etsy or your own website.

Example: A graphic designer might sell social media templates or printable planners. These digital products are popular among bloggers and small business owners looking for time-saving tools.

4. Membership and Subscription Models

Membership and subscription models provide recurring revenue by offering exclusive content or benefits to paying subscribers.

A. Patreon

Patreon allows creators to offer exclusive content to subscribers who pledge monthly support. This can include behind-the-scenes access, early content releases, or exclusive videos.

Example: A podcast might offer bonus episodes or Q&A sessions to Patreon supporters, generating a steady stream of income from loyal fans.

B. Membership Sites

Create a membership site where users pay a monthly or annual fee to access premium content, courses, or community forums. This model works well for niches with dedicated audiences.

Example: A business coach might create a membership site offering monthly webinars, downloadable resources, and a private community for entrepreneurs. Members pay a subscription fee for ongoing access to these resources.

5. Merchandise Sales

Selling branded merchandise allows you to monetise your audience while promoting your brand. Print-on-demand services like Teespring, Printful, and Merch by Amazon make it easy to create and sell custom products without holding inventory.

Example: A popular YouTuber might sell branded t-shirts, mugs, or phone cases featuring their logo or catchphrases. Fans love to support their favourite creators by purchasing merchandise.

6. Crowdfunding and Donations

Crowdfunding and donations can provide financial support from your audience, allowing you to focus on creating high-quality content.

A. Crowdfunding Campaigns

Platforms like Kickstarter and Indiegogo enable you to raise funds for specific projects or products. Successful campaigns offer compelling rewards to backers.

Example: An indie game developer might launch a Kickstarter campaign to fund the development of a new game. By offering early access or exclusive in-game items, they can attract backers and raise the necessary funds.

B. Donations

Accepting donations from your audience can provide financial support, especially if you create valuable free content. Platforms like PayPal, Buy Me a Coffee, and Ko-fi make it easy to accept donations.

Example: A blogger who provides free, high-quality content might add a donation button to their site. Loyal readers who appreciate the content can contribute financially.

Chapter Conclusion

Monetising your digital media efforts requires a strategic approach and a deep understanding of your audience. By exploring various monetisation methods, you can diversify your income streams and maximise your earning potential. Whether through advertising, affiliate marketing, digital product sales, membership models, merchandise, or crowdfunding, the key is to find the strategies that align with your brand and resonate with your audience.

In the next chapter, we will explore how to leverage technology to enhance your digital media efforts. From SEO and analytics to automation tools and AI, we'll discuss how to use technology to streamline your workflow and amplify your success. The digital gold rush is not just about creating content but also about using the right tools to optimise and scale your efforts.

Chapter 5: Leveraging Technology to Amplify Success

In the fast-paced world of digital media, leveraging technology is crucial for streamlining workflows, optimising content, and maximising reach. This chapter will delve into various technological tools and strategies that can help you enhance your digital media efforts. From SEO and analytics to automation tools and AI, we'll explore how to use technology to achieve greater efficiency and success.

1. Search Engine Optimisation (SEO)

SEO is the practice of optimising your content to rank higher in search engine results pages (SERPs), driving organic traffic to your website or content. Here are key components of effective SEO:

A. Keyword Research

Identify the terms and phrases your target audience is searching for. Tools like Google Keyword Planner, SEMrush, and Ahrefs can help you find relevant keywords with high search volume and low competition.

Example: A food blogger might use keyword research tools to discover popular search terms like "easy vegan recipes" or "quick dinner ideas." Incorporating these keywords into their blog posts can attract more visitors.

B. On-Page SEO

Optimise individual web pages to rank higher and earn more relevant traffic. This includes using keywords in your titles, headings, meta descriptions, and throughout your content. Additionally, ensure your website is mobile-friendly and has fast loading times.

Example: An online store selling handmade jewellery can improve on-page SEO by creating detailed product descriptions with relevant

28

keywords, optimising images, and ensuring a smooth mobile shopping experience.

C. Off-Page SEO

Build your website's authority through backlinks from other reputable sites. This can be achieved through guest blogging, collaborations, and creating shareable content.

Example: A tech reviewer can improve off-page SEO by writing guest posts for popular technology blogs and including links back to their own website.

2. Analytics and Data-Driven Decisions

Analytics tools provide valuable insights into your audience's behaviour and the performance of your content. By analysing this data, you can make informed decisions to improve your strategy.

A. Google Analytics

Google Analytics is a powerful tool for tracking website traffic, user behaviour, and conversion rates. It provides detailed reports on how visitors interact with your site, which pages are most popular, and where your traffic is coming from.

Example: A travel blogger can use Google Analytics to determine which blog posts are driving the most traffic and adjust their content strategy accordingly.

B. Social Media Analytics

Most social media platforms offer analytics tools to track engagement, reach, and audience demographics. Tools like Facebook Insights, Twitter Analytics, and Instagram Insights help you understand how your content performs and who your audience is.

Example: An Instagram influencer can use Instagram Insights to analyse which posts receive the most engagement and what times their audience is most active, allowing them to optimise their posting schedule.

3. Automation Tools

Automation tools save time and increase efficiency by handling repetitive tasks. Here are some key areas where automation can be beneficial:

A. Social Media Scheduling

Tools like Buffer, Hootsuite, and Later allow you to schedule social media posts in advance, ensuring consistent posting without manual effort. These tools often include analytics features to track the performance of your posts.

Example: A fitness coach can schedule a week's worth of workout tips and motivational quotes in advance, freeing up time to focus on client interactions.

B. Email Marketing Automation

Email marketing platforms like Mailchimp, ConvertKit, and ActiveCampaign offer automation features that send personalised emails based on user behaviour. You can set up automated welcome sequences, abandoned cart reminders, and segmented email campaigns.

Example: An e-commerce store can use email automation to send personalised product recommendations based on past purchases, increasing the likelihood of repeat sales.

C. Content Management

Content management systems (CMS) like WordPress, Joomla, and Drupal streamline content creation and publication. Plugins and extensions further enhance functionality, allowing for automated SEO optimisation, social sharing, and more.

Example: A news website can use a CMS to automate the publication of scheduled articles and optimise them for SEO automatically.

4. Artificial Intelligence (AI) and Machine Learning

AI and machine learning are transforming digital media by enabling more personalised and efficient content creation and distribution.

A. Content Creation

AI-powered tools like Jasper and Copy.ai can assist in writing articles, generating social media posts, and creating marketing copy. These tools analyse data to produce content that resonates with your audience.

Example: A marketer can use AI to generate compelling ad copy for a new product launch, saving time and ensuring the content is optimised for engagement.

B. Chatbots and Customer Support

AI-driven chatbots like Chatfuel and ManyChat provide instant customer support on websites and social media platforms. They can handle common queries, guide users through processes, and collect valuable customer data.

Example: An online retailer can use a chatbot to assist customers with product inquiries, track orders, and handle returns, enhancing the customer experience without the need for live agents.

C. Personalised Recommendations

Machine learning algorithms analyse user behaviour to provide personalised content recommendations. This technology is widely used by platforms like Netflix, Amazon, and Spotify.

Example: A streaming service can use machine learning to recommend movies and shows based on a user's viewing history, increasing engagement and user satisfaction.

5. Enhancing Productivity and Collaboration

Technology also plays a crucial role in improving productivity and facilitating collaboration, especially for remote teams.

A. Project Management Tools

Tools like Trello, Asana, and Monday.com help teams organise tasks, set deadlines, and track project progress. These platforms enhance communication and ensure everyone is on the same page.

Example: A digital marketing agency can use Trello to manage client campaigns, assign tasks to team members, and monitor progress, ensuring timely and efficient project completion.

B. Cloud Storage and Collaboration

Services like Google Drive, Dropbox, and OneDrive enable teams to store, share, and collaborate on documents in real-time. This is especially useful for remote teams and freelancers working on joint projects.

Example: A content creation team can use Google Drive to collaborate on articles, share multimedia files, and track edits, making the workflow seamless and efficient.

Chapter Conclusion

Leveraging technology is essential for amplifying success in the digital media landscape. By mastering SEO, utilising analytics, automating repetitive tasks, harnessing the power of AI, and enhancing productivity and collaboration, you can optimise your efforts and achieve greater efficiency and impact. The tools and strategies discussed in this chapter provide a foundation for integrating technology into your digital media strategy, allowing you to focus on what you do best: creating and sharing valuable content.

In the next chapter, we will look at some digital media case studies to help fuel your creative imagination.

Chapter 6: Case Studies of Successful Digital Media Entrepreneurs

In this chapter, we will explore the journeys of several successful digital media entrepreneurs. By examining their paths to success, strategies, and challenges, you can gain valuable insights and inspiration for your own digital media endeavours. Each case study highlights different aspects of digital media, from content creation and community building to monetisation and adapting to trends.

Case Study 1: Casey Neistat - Vlogging and Personal Branding

Background: Casey Neistat, a filmmaker and vlogger, is known for his daily vlogs that capture his life and adventures in New York City. He started his YouTube channel in 2010 and quickly gained a massive following due to his unique storytelling style and high-quality production.

Key Strategies:

- **Authenticity:** Neistat's vlogs are known for their authenticity and personal touch. He shares his real-life experiences, thoughts, and emotions, which resonate deeply with his audience.

- **Consistent Posting:** By committing to daily vlogs, Neistat created a routine that kept his audience engaged and coming back for more.

- **Innovative Storytelling:** He uses creative editing techniques, time-lapses, and engaging narratives to make his vlogs stand out.

- **Collaborations:** Neistat frequently collaborates with other creators and brands, expanding his reach and introducing his content to new audiences.

33

Challenges:

- **Burnout:** The intense schedule of daily vlogging led to burnout, prompting Neistat to take breaks and eventually stop daily vlogs.

- **Balancing Privacy:** Sharing personal life online required careful balancing to maintain privacy while still being authentic.

Outcome: Neistat's vlogs have amassed millions of views, leading to brand partnerships, a successful app launch (Beme), and significant influence in the digital media space. He remains a prominent figure in the vlogging community.

Case Study 2: Jenna Marbles - Evolution and Adaptation

Background: Jenna Marbles, one of YouTube's earliest stars, started her channel in 2010 with humorous and relatable content. Her video "How To Trick People Into Thinking You're Good Looking" went viral, propelling her to fame.

Key Strategies:

- **Relatability:** Marbles' content is known for being relatable and humorous, addressing everyday situations and quirks.

- **Diverse Content:** She experimented with various content types, including DIY projects, challenges, and commentary videos.

- **Engagement:** Marbles maintained a strong connection with her audience by responding to comments and incorporating viewer suggestions into her content.

- **Adaptation:** Over the years, she adapted her content to reflect her personal growth and changes in interests, keeping her channel fresh and relevant.

Challenges:

- **Controversies:** Marbles faced backlash for some older videos, prompting her to address the issues publicly and take accountability.

- **Content Evolution:** As she evolved personally, ensuring her content evolved with her audience's expectations was a challenge.

Outcome: Marbles built a loyal following with millions of subscribers. Her adaptability and transparency with her audience contributed to her long-term success. In 2020, she decided to take an indefinite hiatus from YouTube, but her influence and impact on digital media remain significant.

Case Study 3: Pat Flynn - Podcasting and Passive Income

Background: Pat Flynn is the founder of Smart Passive Income, a blog and podcast that provides advice on online business and passive income strategies. He started his journey after being laid off from his job as an architect.

Key Strategies:

- **Educational Content:** Flynn focused on providing valuable, actionable advice for aspiring entrepreneurs, establishing himself as an authority in the niche.

- **Transparency:** He openly shared his income reports and business strategies, building trust and credibility with his audience.

- **Diversification:** Flynn diversified his content across blogs, podcasts, YouTube videos, and online courses.

- **Community Building:** He created a supportive community around his brand through forums, social media groups, and live events.

Challenges:

- **Initial Uncertainty:** Transitioning from a traditional job to an online business was challenging, requiring significant learning and adaptation.

- **Maintaining Quality:** As his content offerings expanded, maintaining high quality and consistency was crucial.

Outcome: Flynn's Smart Passive Income brand has grown into a multi-million-dollar business. His podcast has millions of downloads, and he has successfully launched several online courses and books. Flynn's transparent and educational approach has made him a respected figure in the online business community.

Case Study 4: Lilly Singh - Comedy and Mainstream Success

Background: Lilly Singh, also known as Superwoman, started her YouTube channel in 2010 with comedic skits and relatable content about her Indian heritage and everyday life. Her vibrant personality and humorous takes on cultural issues quickly gained traction.

Key Strategies:

- **Cultural Relevance:** Singh's content often touches on cultural identity, resonating with a diverse audience.

- **High Energy and Humour:** Her energetic and humorous style makes her videos highly engaging.

- **Brand Extensions:** Singh expanded her brand into merchandise, a book deal, a world tour, and a late-night television show.

- **Social Issues:** She uses her platform to address important social issues, increasing her impact and relevance.

Challenges:

- **Burnout:** The pressure of constant content creation and maintaining high energy led to periods of burnout.

- **Transitioning to Mainstream:** Moving from YouTube to mainstream television presented new challenges and required different strategies.

Outcome: Singh has over 14 million subscribers on YouTube and has successfully transitioned to mainstream media with her late-night show, "A Little Late with Lilly Singh." Her ability to leverage her online success into other opportunities has solidified her as a versatile and influential media personality.

Case Study 5: Marques Brownlee - Tech Reviews and Expertise

Background: Marques Brownlee, known as MKBHD, started his YouTube channel in 2008, focusing on tech reviews and tutorials. His detailed and high-quality content quickly set him apart in the tech community.

Key Strategies:

- **Expertise:** Brownlee's deep knowledge of technology and attention to detail establish him as an expert in the field.

- **High Production Value:** Investing in top-notch equipment and editing techniques has made his videos visually appealing and professional.

- **Consistency:** Regularly posting well-researched and comprehensive reviews has built a loyal following.

- **Industry Connections:** Building relationships with tech companies and influencers has provided access to exclusive products and collaborations.

Challenges:

- **Staying Updated:** Keeping up with rapidly evolving technology and maintaining relevance requires continuous learning and adaptation.

- **Balancing Depth and Accessibility:** Ensuring content is detailed enough for tech enthusiasts but accessible to general viewers.

Outcome: Brownlee's channel has over 16 million subscribers, and he is widely regarded as one of the top tech reviewers on YouTube. His success has led to interviews with tech industry leaders and appearances on mainstream media, solidifying his status as a leading authority in tech media.

Chapter Conclusion

These case studies highlight the diverse paths to success in digital media. Whether through vlogging, podcasting, comedy, tech reviews, or personal branding, each entrepreneur leveraged their unique strengths, embraced authenticity, and adapted to the evolving digital landscape.

By learning from their experiences, you can gain valuable insights and strategies to apply to your own journey. Remember, success in digital media is not a one-size-fits-all approach. It requires passion, creativity, perseverance, and a willingness to evolve. Embrace your unique voice, create valuable content, engage with your community, and stay adaptable to the ever-changing digital media landscape. Your path to success is yours to create, and the possibilities are endless.

In the next chapter, we will discuss how to overcome challenges and setbacks in your digital media journey. From managing burnout and handling negative feedback to navigating algorithm changes and competition, we'll explore strategies to maintain resilience and stay on the path to success. The digital gold rush is filled with opportunities, but it also requires perseverance and adaptability to thrive in an ever-changing landscape.

Chapter 7: Challenges and Pitfalls

The digital media industry offers vast opportunities but also presents several challenges and pitfalls that can hinder success. Understanding and addressing these issues is crucial for sustainable growth and long-term success. This chapter will discuss some of the most common challenges in digital media, including platform dependency, burnout, and maintaining relevance. Additionally, strategies for overcoming these challenges will be provided.

Platform Dependency

One of the significant risks for digital media creators is becoming overly reliant on a single platform. This dependency can be problematic because changes in algorithms, policies, or platform popularity can drastically affect your reach and income.

Challenges:

- **Algorithm Changes:** Social media platforms like Facebook, Instagram, and YouTube frequently update their algorithms, which can reduce the visibility of your content.

- **Policy Changes:** Shifts in platform policies can impact content monetisation and distribution.

- **Platform Popularity:** The rise and fall of social media platforms can lead to audience migration, affecting your follower base and engagement.

Strategies to Overcome Platform Dependency:

1. **Diversify Your Platforms:**
   - Expand your presence across multiple social media platforms to reduce risk.

- Tailor content strategies to leverage the strengths of each platform.

2. **Build Your Own Channels:**

   - Develop a personal website and email newsletter to have direct access to your audience.

   - Use these channels to distribute content, share updates, and foster a community.

3. **Stay Informed and Adaptable:**

   - Keep up with platform changes and industry news to quickly adapt your strategies.

   - Experiment with new platforms and technologies to stay ahead of trends.

Burnout

Creating and managing digital content can be demanding, often leading to burnout. This is particularly challenging for solo creators or small teams who handle all aspects of content creation and management.

Challenges:

- **Constant Content Creation:** The pressure to consistently produce high-quality content can lead to exhaustion.

- **Work-Life Balance:** Managing multiple tasks and maintaining an online presence can blur the lines between personal and professional life.

- **Mental Health:** The continuous demand for content and interaction with the audience can take a toll on mental health.

Strategies to Overcome Burnout:

1. **Set Realistic Goals:**

   o   Establish achievable content schedules and allow time for breaks.

   o   Focus on quality over quantity to maintain a sustainable pace.

2. **Delegate and Collaborate:**

   o   Outsource tasks such as editing, graphic design, or social media management.

   o   Collaborate with other creators to share the workload and bring fresh perspectives.

3. **Practice Self-Care:**

   o   Incorporate regular breaks, exercise, and hobbies into your routine.

   o   Seek support from friends, family, or professionals when needed.

4. **Automate and Streamline:**

   o   Use tools to automate repetitive tasks and streamline your workflow.

   o   Plan and schedule content in advance to reduce daily stress.

Maintaining Relevance

In the fast-paced digital world, staying relevant requires continuous innovation and adaptation. Audience interests can shift rapidly, and new competitors emerge frequently.

Challenges:

- **Content Fatigue:** Audiences may lose interest if content becomes repetitive or stagnant.

- **Increased Competition:** New creators and changing trends can overshadow established brands.

- **Evolving Trends:** Keeping up with the latest trends and technologies requires constant effort.

Strategies to Maintain Relevance:

1. **Continuous Learning:**

   o Invest time in learning new skills, tools, and trends.

   o Attend industry events, webinars, and workshops to stay updated.

2. **Engage with Your Audience:**

   o Solicit feedback to understand your audience's evolving interests.

   o Use interactive content like polls, Q&A sessions, and live streams to foster engagement.

3. **Experiment with Content:**

   o Introduce new formats, themes, and collaborations to keep content fresh.

   o Analyse performance data to identify successful content and refine your strategy.

4. **Build a Strong Brand:**

   o Develop a distinct voice, style, and value proposition that sets you apart.

o   Consistently communicate your brand values to build a loyal audience.

Chapter Conclusion

The digital media industry presents numerous challenges and pitfalls, but with the right strategies, they can be effectively navigated. By diversifying platform presence, managing burnout, and staying relevant through continuous learning and audience engagement, you can build a resilient and successful digital media career. Embrace these strategies to turn challenges into opportunities, ensuring long-term success in the dynamic world of digital media.

In the next chapter, we will discuss the future of digital media and emerging trends. Staying ahead of the curve and adapting to new technologies and trends is crucial for long-term success. We'll explore upcoming innovations, shifts in consumer behaviour, and how to position yourself for continued growth in the ever-evolving digital landscape.

Chapter 8: The Future of Digital Media

The digital media landscape is constantly evolving, shaped by technological advancements, shifting consumer behaviours, and emerging opportunities. This chapter will provide a forward-looking perspective on where digital media is headed, exploring the impact of new technologies, changes in audience engagement, and potential new avenues for growth.

The Impact of New Technologies

Technological innovation is a driving force behind the evolution of digital media. Emerging technologies are transforming how content is created, distributed, and consumed.

Artificial Intelligence (AI) and Machine Learning:

- **Content Creation and Curation:** AI tools can assist in creating content, from writing articles to generating visuals and videos. Machine learning algorithms help curate personalised content for users, enhancing engagement.

- **Analytics and Insights:** AI-driven analytics provide deeper insights into audience behaviour, allowing for more effective content strategies and targeted marketing.

Virtual Reality (VR) and Augmented Reality (AR):

- **Immersive Experiences:** VR and AR are creating new opportunities for immersive storytelling and interactive content. Brands can engage audiences through virtual tours, 360-degree videos, and AR-enhanced products.

- **Gaming and Entertainment:** These technologies are revolutionising the gaming industry and are being integrated into entertainment platforms for more engaging experiences.

Blockchain Technology:

- **Content Monetisation:** Blockchain offers new ways to monetise content through decentralised platforms and secure payment systems. It also ensures transparent and fair revenue distribution for creators.

- **Digital Ownership:** Non-fungible tokens (NFTs) enable digital ownership of unique content, providing new revenue streams for creators and fostering a sense of exclusivity and value.

Evolving Consumer Behaviours

Consumer behaviours and preferences are continuously changing, influenced by technological advancements and societal trends.

On-Demand Content:

- **Streaming Services:** The shift towards on-demand content is evident in the rise of streaming platforms like Netflix, YouTube, and Twitch. Audiences prefer to consume content at their convenience, driving the demand for binge-worthy series and live streaming.

- **Short-Form Content:** Platforms like TikTok and Instagram Reels cater to the growing preference for short, engaging content. Creators need to adapt by producing concise and impactful videos.

Mobile-First Consumption:

- **Smartphone Dominance:** With the increasing use of smartphones, mobile-first content is essential. Optimising content for mobile devices, including responsive design and mobile-friendly interfaces, is crucial for reaching a wider audience.

- **Social Media Integration:** Consumers spend significant time on social media apps, making these platforms critical for content distribution and engagement.

Interactive and Participatory Content:

- **User-Generated Content (UGC):** Encouraging UGC fosters community engagement and builds authenticity. Brands and creators can leverage UGC for marketing and audience building.

- **Interactive Experiences:** Interactive content, such as quizzes, polls, and live Q&A sessions, enhances user engagement and creates a more personalised experience.

Potential New Opportunities

The future of digital media presents numerous opportunities for innovation and growth. Embracing these trends can position creators and brands at the forefront of the industry.

Niche Content and Communities:

- **Specialised Platforms:** As mainstream platforms become saturated, there is a growing demand for niche platforms catering to specific interests and communities. Creating content for these platforms can lead to highly engaged and loyal audiences.

- **Community Building:** Fostering strong, interactive communities around specific topics or interests can drive long-term engagement and support.

Hybrid Events and Experiences:

- **Virtual and In-Person Integration:** The rise of virtual events during the pandemic has led to the popularity of hybrid events, combining virtual and in-person experiences. This model allows for broader audience reach and more flexible participation options.

- **Augmented Reality Experiences:** Incorporating AR into events and experiences can enhance engagement and provide unique, interactive opportunities for attendees.

Ethical and Inclusive Content:

- **Diverse Representation:** Audiences are increasingly seeking content that reflects diverse perspectives and experiences. Prioritising diversity and inclusion in content creation can attract a broader audience and foster positive brand perception.

- **Ethical Practices:** Transparency, authenticity, and ethical practices are becoming essential for building trust with audiences. Brands and creators who prioritise these values will likely see increased loyalty and support.

Chapter Conclusion

The future of digital media is shaped by rapid technological advancements, evolving consumer behaviours, and emerging opportunities. By staying ahead of these trends and adapting to changes, creators and brands can thrive in this dynamic landscape. Embracing new technologies, understanding shifting audience preferences, and exploring innovative opportunities will ensure continued growth and relevance in the ever-evolving world of digital media.

In the next chapter we will look more in depth at some of the emerging trends and their key aspects.

Chapter 9: Emerging Trends in Digital Media

The digital media landscape is continually evolving, driven by advancements in technology, shifts in consumer behaviour, and the emergence of new trends. Staying ahead of these trends is crucial for digital media creators and brands to remain relevant and successful. This chapter explores some of the most significant emerging trends, including short-form content, the role of AR/VR, AI's impact on personalisation, the benefits of live streaming, data privacy concerns, platform diversification, and other key developments shaping the future of digital media.

Short-Form Content

Short-form content has become a dominant force in digital media, thanks to platforms like TikTok, Instagram Reels, and YouTube Shorts. This format caters to the fast-paced consumption habits of modern audiences, offering quick, engaging, and easily digestible content.

Key Aspects:

- **Bite-Sized Information:** Delivering concise and impactful messages within a short time frame.

- **Creative Formats:** Utilising trends, challenges, and music to make content more engaging.

- **Cross-Platform Sharing:** Repurposing short-form content across different platforms to maximise reach and engagement.

The Role of AR/VR

Augmented Reality (AR) and Virtual Reality (VR) are revolutionising the digital media experience by providing immersive and interactive content. These technologies are transforming how audiences engage with content, from virtual tours to interactive storytelling.

Key Aspects:

- **Enhanced Storytelling:** Using AR and VR to create immersive narratives that engage users on a deeper level.

- **Virtual Experiences:** Offering virtual events, product demos, and 360-degree videos to provide unique experiences.

- **Interactive Marketing:** Implementing AR filters and VR experiences in marketing campaigns to captivate audiences and boost engagement.

AI's Impact on Personalisation

Artificial Intelligence (AI) is significantly enhancing the personalisation of content and user experiences. By analysing user data, AI can deliver tailored content recommendations, improve targeting, and optimise engagement.

Key Aspects:

- **Content Recommendations:** Leveraging AI algorithms to suggest personalised content based on user preferences and behaviour.

- **Chatbots and Virtual Assistants:** Using AI-powered chatbots to provide personalised customer service and support.

- **Predictive Analytics:** Employing AI to analyse trends and predict future content performance, aiding in strategic planning.

The Benefits of Live Streaming

Live streaming has become a vital component of digital media, offering real-time interaction and engagement. Platforms like Twitch, YouTube Live, and Facebook Live have made live streaming accessible to a broad audience.

Key Aspects:

- **Real-Time Engagement:** Using live streaming to interact directly with your audience, answer questions, and receive immediate feedback.

- **Events and Webinars:** Hosting live events, webinars, and Q&A sessions to provide valuable content and build community.

- **Collaborations:** Partnering with other creators or brands for joint live streams to reach new audiences and create dynamic content.

Data Privacy Concerns

With increasing concerns about data privacy, digital media creators and platforms must prioritise user data protection and transparency. Trust and ethical practices are becoming essential for maintaining audience loyalty.

Key Aspects:

- **Transparent Policies:** Clearly communicating data collection and usage policies to your audience.

- **Data Protection:** Implementing robust security measures to protect user data and prevent breaches.

- **Consent Management:** Ensuring that users have control over their data and can easily manage their privacy settings.

Platform Diversification

Relying on a single platform can be risky due to algorithm changes and policy shifts. Diversifying your presence across multiple platforms can mitigate these risks and expand your reach.

Key Aspects:

- **Cross-Platform Strategy:** Developing a cohesive strategy that leverages the unique strengths of each platform.

- **Consistent Branding:** Maintaining consistent branding and messaging across all platforms to build a strong identity.

- **Audience Engagement:** Tailoring content and engagement strategies to the specific audiences of each platform.

Other Emerging Trends

The digital media industry is constantly evolving, with new trends shaping its future. Staying ahead of these trends is crucial for success.

Key Emerging Trends:

- **Voice Search and Smart Speakers:** Optimising content for voice search and exploring opportunities with smart speaker platforms like Amazon Alexa and Google Home.

- **Blockchain and NFTs:** Exploring the potential of blockchain technology and non-fungible tokens (NFTs) for content monetisation and digital ownership.

- **Sustainability and Ethics:** Emphasising sustainable practices and ethical content creation to appeal to environmentally and socially conscious audiences.

- **Interactive Content:** Incorporating interactive elements such as polls, quizzes, and clickable videos to enhance user engagement.

- **Micro-Influencers:** Collaborating with micro-influencers who have highly engaged, niche audiences for more authentic and targeted marketing.

Chapter Conclusion

The future of digital media is dynamic and full of opportunities. By embracing short-form content, leveraging AR/VR, utilising AI for personalisation, capitalising on live streaming, addressing data privacy concerns, diversifying platforms, and staying attuned to emerging trends, creators and brands can thrive in this ever-changing landscape. Adaptability, innovation, and a focus on audience needs will be key to sustaining growth and success in the digital media world.

In the following chapter we will cover essential business practices, growth strategies, and the importance of staying ahead of industry trends.

Chapter 10: Building a Sustainable Digital Media Business

In the final chapter, we will delve into the critical elements necessary for sustaining long-term success in the digital media landscape. Building a profitable digital media business is not just about achieving quick wins; it requires strategic planning, adaptability, and a commitment to continuous improvement.

Business Planning and Strategy

To create a sustainable digital media business, having a solid business plan is crucial. This includes defining your goals, understanding your market, and developing a clear strategy for growth.

Key Aspects:

- **Defining Objectives:** Establish clear, measurable goals for your digital media business, such as revenue targets, audience growth, and engagement metrics.

- **Market Analysis:** Conduct thorough research to understand your target audience, competitors, and market trends. This information will inform your content and marketing strategies.

- **Strategic Planning:** Develop a comprehensive plan that outlines your business model, revenue streams, marketing tactics, and growth initiatives.

Scaling Your Business

Growth is a critical component of a sustainable digital media business. Scaling effectively requires leveraging technology, building a team, and continuously innovating your content and marketing strategies.

Key Aspects:

- **Leveraging Technology:** Use tools and platforms to automate processes, enhance productivity, and scale your content distribution. Examples include social media schedulers, analytics tools, and customer relationship management (CRM) systems.

- **Team Building:** As your business grows, consider expanding your team to include content creators, marketers, and technical experts. This will allow you to focus on strategic initiatives and business development.

- **Content Innovation:** Continuously experiment with new content formats, platforms, and engagement techniques to keep your audience interested and attract new followers.

Financial Management

Effective financial management is essential for sustaining and growing your digital media business. This involves budgeting, diversifying revenue streams, and investing in growth opportunities.

Key Aspects:

- **Budgeting and Forecasting:** Create detailed budgets and financial forecasts to manage your expenses and plan for future investments.

- **Revenue Diversification:** Explore multiple revenue streams to reduce dependency on any single source. This can include ad revenue, sponsored content, merchandise sales, subscriptions, and more.

- **Investment in Growth:** Allocate funds for marketing, technology upgrades, and team expansion to support ongoing growth and development.

Legal and Ethical Considerations

Navigating the legal and ethical aspects of digital media is crucial for long-term success. This includes protecting your intellectual property, complying with regulations, and maintaining ethical standards in your content and business practices.

Key Aspects:

- **Intellectual Property Protection:** Ensure that your content and brand assets are protected by trademarks, copyrights, or patents where applicable.

- **Regulatory Compliance:** Stay informed about relevant regulations and industry standards, such as data privacy laws (e.g., GDPR) and advertising guidelines.

- **Ethical Standards:** Commit to ethical content creation and business practices, including transparency, honesty, and respect for your audience and collaborators.

Staying Ahead of Industry Trends

The digital media landscape is constantly evolving. Staying informed about emerging trends and adapting your strategies accordingly is essential for maintaining relevance and competitive advantage.

Key Aspects:

- **Continuous Learning:** Regularly update your knowledge and skills through courses, workshops, and industry events.

- **Trend Monitoring:** Keep an eye on industry reports, news, and thought leaders to stay informed about the latest developments and opportunities.

- **Adaptability:** Be willing to pivot your strategies and explore new opportunities as the digital media landscape evolves.

Chapter Conclusion

Building a sustainable digital media business requires a strategic approach, continuous innovation, and a commitment to ethical practices. By focusing on business planning, scaling effectively, managing finances wisely, navigating legal and ethical considerations, and staying ahead of industry trends, you can create a thriving digital media enterprise that stands the test of time. The journey to becoming a digital media millionaire is challenging but achievable with the right mindset, tools, and strategies.

Conclusion: Your Path to Success in Digital Media

Embarking on a journey in digital media is an exciting and dynamic endeavour. The landscape is constantly evolving, offering endless opportunities for creativity, engagement, and monetisation. As we conclude this book, let's reflect on the key insights and strategies that can guide you towards a successful and fulfilling career in digital media.

1. Embrace Your Unique Voice and Niche

Success in digital media starts with understanding and embracing your unique voice and niche. Whether you're a blogger, vlogger, podcaster, or social media influencer, your individuality sets you apart.

A. Find Your Passion

Identify what you're passionate about and what you can consistently create content around. Passion drives creativity and helps you stay motivated through the challenges.

B. Define Your Niche

Narrowing down your niche allows you to target a specific audience and become an authority in that area. The more focused your niche, the more you can cater to the needs and interests of your audience.

2. Create High-Quality, Valuable Content

Content is the cornerstone of digital media. High-quality, valuable content attracts and retains an audience, builds trust, and establishes your brand.

A. Focus on Quality

Invest time and effort into creating polished, well-researched, and visually appealing content. Quality content stands out and resonates with your audience.

B. Provide Value

Think about what your audience needs and how you can help them. Valuable content solves problems, entertains, educates, or inspires.

3. Engage and Build a Community

Engagement is key to building a loyal and active community. Your audience is not just passive consumers but active participants in your journey.

A. Foster Interaction

Encourage comments, questions, and discussions. Respond to your audience, show appreciation, and make them feel valued.

B. Create a Sense of Belonging

Cultivate a sense of community by creating content that resonates with your audience's values and interests. Exclusive content, live interactions, and community events can strengthen these bonds.

4. Diversify Your Income Streams

Monetising your digital presence requires a strategic approach and diversification. Relying on a single income stream can be risky.

A. Explore Various Revenue Streams

Ad revenue, sponsorships, merchandise, and crowdfunding are just a few ways to monetise your content. Each income stream has its own benefits and challenges.

B. Balance Monetisation and User Experience

Ensure that your monetisation strategies do not compromise the user experience. Prioritise providing value while finding ways to monetise ethically and sustainably.

5. Stay Adaptable and Ahead of Trends

The digital media landscape is ever-changing. Staying adaptable and ahead of trends is crucial for long-term success.

A. Embrace New Technologies

Stay informed about emerging technologies like AR, VR, and AI. Experiment with new formats and platforms to keep your content fresh and engaging.

B. Monitor Trends

Keep an eye on industry trends and consumer behaviour. Adapt your strategies to stay relevant and meet the evolving needs of your audience.

6. Prioritise Ethical Practices and Data Privacy

In a world where data privacy and ethical considerations are paramount, building trust with your audience is essential.

A. Protect User Data

Ensure that you comply with data privacy regulations and protect your audience's data. Transparency and integrity are crucial.

B. Create Ethically

Avoid spreading misinformation, respect intellectual property, and maintain honesty in your content and interactions.

7. Learn from Successful Case Studies

Real-world examples of successful digital media entrepreneurs can provide valuable insights and inspiration. Learning from their journeys can help you navigate your own path.

A. Study Success Stories

Look at how successful creators built their brands, overcame challenges, and achieved success. Adapt their strategies to your own context.

B. Apply Lessons Learned

Take actionable insights from case studies and apply them to your own digital media endeavours. Continuous learning and adaptation are key.

Final Thoughts

Your journey in digital media is unique and filled with potential. By embracing your voice, creating valuable content, engaging with your audience, diversifying your income, staying adaptable, prioritising ethics, and learning from others, you can build a successful and fulfilling career.

Remember, success in digital media is not just about the numbers. It's about the impact you have on your audience, the community you build, and the passion you bring to your work. Stay true to your vision, keep evolving, and enjoy the journey.

Thank you for joining us on this exploration of the digital media landscape. We wish you all the best in your future endeavours and hope this book serves as a valuable guide on your path to success.

Appendix 1: Three Example Approaches to Get Started

Embarking on a journey in digital media can seem daunting, but by following proven approaches and examples, you can set yourself up for success. Here are three practical examples and approaches to help you get started in the digital media industry.

Example 1: Launching a Niche YouTube Channel

Focus Area: Identify a Specific Niche with a Dedicated Audience

Starting a YouTube channel in a specific niche is a strategic move that can lead to a dedicated and engaged audience. Popular niches include tech reviews, travel vlogging, DIY crafts, beauty and makeup tutorials, and gaming. Choosing a niche that aligns with your passion and expertise will make content creation more enjoyable and sustainable, as you'll be motivated to consistently produce high-quality content. Here are the detailed steps to get started:

Steps to Get Started:

1. Market Research:

- **Analyse Existing Channels:** Begin by researching existing YouTube channels in your chosen niche. Pay attention to successful channels and identify what makes them popular. Look at their content type, style, video length, and posting frequency.

- **Identify Gaps:** Look for gaps in content that you can fill. This might include underserved topics, new trends, or a different approach to common subjects. For example, if you're interested in tech reviews, you might notice a lack of in-depth reviews for budget gadgets.

- **Audience Insights:** Use tools like YouTube Analytics and Google Trends to understand what viewers are searching for and which videos are trending. This data can help you tailor your content to meet audience demand.

2. Content Planning:

- **Develop a Content Calendar:** Plan your content in advance to ensure consistency. A content calendar helps you organise your ideas and maintain a regular posting schedule. Include a mix of video types such as tutorials, reviews, vlogs, and Q&A sessions to keep your audience engaged.

- **Balance Content Types:** Balance evergreen content (which remains relevant over time) with timely content (which capitalises on current trends). For instance, in a beauty channel, evergreen content might include makeup tutorials, while timely content could feature seasonal looks or new product launches.

- **Plan for Engagement:** Think about ways to interact with your audience. This could include live streams, responding to comments, or creating community posts.

3. Equipment and Setup:

- **Basic Equipment:** Invest in essential video recording equipment such as a good quality camera, a reliable microphone, and proper lighting. These tools will significantly enhance your video quality, making your channel more professional.

- **Set Design:** Create a visually appealing set or backdrop for your videos. This doesn't have to be elaborate but should reflect your niche and personality. For example, a tech review channel might feature a clean, modern setup with gadgets in the background.

- **Editing Software:** Use video editing software to polish your videos. Basic tools like iMovie or Windows Movie Maker are good starting points, but as you grow, consider investing in more advanced software like Adobe Premiere Pro or Final Cut Pro.

4. SEO and Optimisation:

- **Optimise Video Titles:** Craft compelling and descriptive titles that include relevant keywords. A good title not only helps with SEO but also entices viewers to click on your video.

- **Descriptions and Tags:** Write detailed descriptions that provide context for your video and include key phrases viewers might be searching for. Use tags to help YouTube's algorithm understand your video's content and recommend it to relevant audiences.

- **Engaging Thumbnails:** Create custom thumbnails that are eye-catching and relevant to your video. Thumbnails play a crucial role in attracting viewers, so make sure they are visually appealing and professionally designed.

5. Monetisation:

- **YouTube Partner Program:** Once you meet YouTube's eligibility criteria (typically 1,000 subscribers and 4,000 watch hours in the past 12 months), you can apply for the YouTube Partner Program to start earning ad revenue.

- **Sponsored Content:** As your channel grows, brands may approach you for sponsored content. Ensure any sponsorship aligns with your niche and is something your audience will find valuable.

- **Affiliate Marketing:** Promote products relevant to your niche and earn a commission on sales through affiliate marketing. Include affiliate links in your video descriptions.

- **Merchandise Sales:** Consider creating and selling your own merchandise. Platforms like Teespring allow you to design and sell products like t-shirts, mugs, and more.

- **Subscription Models:** Platforms like Patreon enable creators to offer exclusive content to subscribers for a monthly fee. This can include behind-the-scenes videos, early access to new content, or personalised shout-outs.

By following these steps, you can effectively launch and grow a niche YouTube channel. Remember, the key to success is consistency, high-quality content, and engaging with your audience. As you build your channel, continuously seek feedback and be willing to adapt and improve your strategies.

Success Story: Marques Brownlee, known as MKBHD, started his YouTube channel with simple tech reviews filmed in his bedroom. Through consistent high-quality content and in-depth reviews, he has grown to become one of the most respected tech reviewers on the platform, with millions of subscribers and significant earnings from various monetisation strategies.

Example 2: Building an Influential Blog

Focus Area: Choose a Niche You Are Passionate About and Knowledgeable In

Starting a blog can be a rewarding venture, especially when you focus on a niche that aligns with your passions and expertise. Popular blog niches include personal finance, health and wellness, fashion, parenting, and food. A well-defined niche helps attract a dedicated readership and allows you to establish yourself as an authority in that field. Here are the detailed steps to get started:

Steps to Get Started:

1. Domain and Hosting:

- **Purchase a Domain Name:** Choose a domain name that reflects your blog's niche and brand. It should be easy to remember, spell, and type. A good domain name is crucial for creating a strong online identity.

- **Choose a Reliable Hosting Service:** Select a hosting provider that offers good performance, reliability, and customer support. Popular options include Bluehost, SiteGround, and WP Engine. Your hosting service ensures your blog runs smoothly and is accessible to readers.

- **Set Up Your Blog Platform:** Install a blogging platform like WordPress, which offers user-friendly features and a wide range of themes and plugins to customise your blog.

2. Content Strategy:

- **Plan Your Content:** Develop a content calendar to organise your post ideas and schedule. Aim to publish consistently, whether weekly, bi-weekly, or monthly. Consistent posting helps keep your readers engaged and improves your blog's SEO.

- **Mix of Content Types:** Create a variety of posts, including informative articles, how-to guides, personal stories, and listicles. This variety keeps your content fresh and engaging.

- **Evergreen Content:** Focus on creating evergreen content that remains relevant over time. Topics that provide long-lasting value will continue to attract readers and traffic long after they are published.

- **High-Quality and Well-Researched Posts:** Ensure your posts are well-written, thoroughly researched, and provide valuable insights. High-quality content establishes your authority and encourages readers to return.

3. SEO Practices:

- **Keyword Research:** Use keyword research tools like Google Keyword Planner, Ahrefs, or SEMrush to identify relevant keywords for your niche. Incorporate these keywords naturally into your blog posts.

- **Optimise Posts:** Optimise your posts with on-page SEO techniques, such as using keywords in titles, headings, meta descriptions, and alt text for images. Ensure your posts are well-structured and easy to read.

- **Internal and External Links:** Include internal links to other relevant posts on your blog and external links to authoritative sources. This improves your SEO and provides additional value to your readers.

- **Speed and Mobile Optimisation:** Ensure your blog loads quickly and is mobile-friendly. Use tools like Google PageSpeed Insights to check your blog's performance and make necessary improvements.

4. Audience Engagement:

- **Engage with Readers:** Respond to comments on your blog posts to build a sense of community and show that you value reader feedback. Encourage discussions by asking questions and prompting readers to share their thoughts.

- **Social Media Presence:** Promote your blog posts on social media platforms relevant to your niche. Engaging with your audience on social media helps drive traffic to your blog and increases your reach.

- **Email Newsletters:** Build an email list and send regular newsletters to your subscribers. Newsletters keep your audience informed about new posts, updates, and exclusive content.

- **Interactive Content:** Include interactive elements like polls, quizzes, and surveys to engage your readers and gather valuable feedback.

5. Monetisation:

- **Display Ads:** Sign up for advertising networks like Google AdSense to display ads on your blog. Earnings are based on the number of impressions and clicks on the ads.

- **Sponsored Posts:** Collaborate with brands to create sponsored content. Ensure that sponsored posts align with your niche and provide value to your readers.

- **Affiliate Marketing:** Promote products or services relevant to your niche through affiliate links. Earn a commission for every sale made through your referral.

- **Digital Products and Courses:** Create and sell digital products like e-books, printables, or online courses. This can be a lucrative way to monetise your expertise and provide additional value to your readers.

- **Membership and Subscription Models:** Offer premium content or exclusive access to a members-only section of your blog for a subscription fee. This creates a steady income stream and provides additional value to your most dedicated readers.

By following these steps, you can build an influential blog that attracts a dedicated readership and generates income. Focus on delivering high-quality, valuable content, engaging with your audience, and exploring diverse monetisation strategies to achieve long-term success.

Success Story: Pat Flynn, the founder of Smart Passive Income, started his blog to share his journey and strategies in building online businesses. His transparent approach and valuable content have made him a leading figure in the blogging and online business community, earning a substantial income from various monetisation methods.

Example 3: Creating a Successful Podcast

Focus Area: Identify a Topic or Theme You Are Passionate About with Potential Audience

Creating a podcast can be an excellent way to share your passion and knowledge with a broad audience. To build a successful podcast, choose a topic or theme that you are genuinely passionate about and that resonates with a potential audience. This could range from personal development, true crime, business and entrepreneurship, to entertainment and pop culture. Here are the detailed steps to get started:

Steps to Get Started:

1. Concept and Planning:

- **Define Your Format:** Decide on the format of your podcast. Will it be a solo show, an interview-style podcast, or a panel discussion? Each format has its unique appeal and can attract different types of listeners.

- **Episode Length and Frequency:** Determine the length of your episodes. While some podcasts are successful with short, 10–15 minute episodes, others thrive with longer, 60-90 minute deep dives. Decide how often you will release new episodes (e.g., weekly, bi-weekly, monthly).

- **Content Plan:** Create a content calendar outlining your topics for each episode. Include a mix of solo episodes, interviews with industry experts or interesting guests, and discussions on trending topics within your niche. Planning ahead ensures a steady flow of content and helps maintain consistency.

2. Equipment and Software:

- **Recording Equipment:** Invest in good-quality recording equipment. A high-quality microphone is essential for clear audio, while a pair of headphones helps you monitor the sound. Popular microphones for podcasters include the Blue Yeti, Audio-Technica ATR2100x, and Shure SM7B.

- **Recording Space:** Choose a quiet space with minimal background noise for recording. Consider using soundproofing materials or portable sound booths to improve audio quality.

- **Editing Software:** Use podcast editing software to produce professional-sounding episodes. Audacity and GarageBand are excellent free options, while Adobe Audition and Hindenburg offer more advanced features for a fee.

- **Hosting Platform:** Select a podcast hosting platform that suits your needs. Popular choices include Libsyn, Podbean, and Anchor. These platforms will distribute your episodes to major podcast directories like Apple Podcasts, Spotify, and Google Podcasts.

3. Branding and Marketing:

- **Develop Your Brand:** Create a strong brand for your podcast. Choose a catchy name that reflects your content and is easy to remember. Design a compelling logo and select theme music that fits your podcast's tone and style.

- **Promote on Social Media:** Utilise social media platforms to promote your podcast. Create profiles on Twitter, Instagram, Facebook, and LinkedIn, and post regularly to engage with potential listeners. Share episode highlights, behind-the-scenes content, and interact with your audience.

- **Build a Website:** Develop a website for your podcast where listeners can find all your episodes, show notes, and additional content. A website also helps with SEO and provides a hub for your online presence.

- **Collaborate with Other Podcasters:** Collaborate with other podcasters in your niche to reach new audiences. Guest appearances, cross-promotions, and shout-outs can help increase your visibility and attract more listeners.

4. Engage with Listeners:

- **Social Media Engagement:** Build a community around your podcast by engaging with listeners on social media. Respond to comments, ask questions, and encourage discussions related to your episodes.

- **Feedback and Reviews:** Encourage listeners to leave reviews and provide feedback. Positive reviews can attract new listeners, while constructive feedback helps you improve your content.

- **Interactive Content:** Create interactive content like Q&A episodes, where you answer questions from your audience. This makes listeners feel valued and part of the podcast community.

- **Listener Involvement:** Consider involving listeners in your episodes. This could be through call-ins, voice messages, or featuring listener stories. Interactive episodes can boost engagement and loyalty.

5. Monetisation:

- **Sponsorship Deals:** As your podcast grows, attract sponsors who want to advertise to your audience. Ensure that sponsorships align with your content and provide value to your listeners.

- **Listener Donations:** Platforms like Patreon allow listeners to support your podcast financially. Offer exclusive content, early access to episodes, or other perks to encourage donations.

- **Affiliate Marketing:** Promote products or services relevant to your niche and earn a commission through affiliate marketing. Mention these products during episodes and include affiliate links in your show notes.

- **Premium Content:** Consider offering premium content behind a paywall. This could include bonus episodes, ad-free listening, or access to a members-only community.

- **Merchandise Sales:** Create and sell merchandise related to your podcast. T-shirts, mugs, and other branded items can provide additional income and help promote your podcast.

By following these steps, you can create a successful podcast that attracts a dedicated audience and generates income. Focus on delivering high-quality, engaging content, actively engaging with your listeners, and exploring diverse monetisation strategies to achieve long-term success.

Success Story: Joe Rogan's "The Joe Rogan Experience" started as a casual podcast and has grown into one of the most popular podcasts in the world. His engaging content, diverse guest list, and unique style have led to significant earnings through sponsorships, ad revenue, and a lucrative exclusive licensing deal with Spotify.

By following these examples and approaches, you can effectively start your journey in the digital media industry. Whether it's through YouTube, blogging, or podcasting, the key to success lies in consistent, high-quality content, audience engagement, and strategic monetisation.

Appendix 2: Useful Resources

Recommended Reading

Expand your knowledge with these recommended books on digital media, entrepreneurship, and personal development:

1. **"Crushing It!: How Great Entrepreneurs Build Their Business and Influence—and How You Can, Too" by Gary Vaynerchuk**

2. **"Contagious: How to Build Word of Mouth in the Digital Age" by Jonah Berger**

3. **"Platform Revolution: How Networked Markets Are Transforming the Economy—and How to Make Them Work for You" by Geoffrey G. Parker, Marshall W. Van Alstyne, and Sangeet Paul Choudary**

4. **"Hooked: How to Build Habit-Forming Products" by Nir Eyal**

5. **"The Lean Startup: How Today's Entrepreneurs Use Continuous Innovation to Create Radically Successful Businesses" by Eric Ries**

Useful Websites

Explore these websites for tools, insights, and communities in digital media and entrepreneurship:

1. **HubSpot Academy** - Offers free courses on digital marketing and content creation.

2. **Social Media Examiner** - Provides tips, strategies, and industry news for social media marketing.

3. **Google Analytics Academy** - Learn how to use Google Analytics to track and analyse website traffic.

4. **Reddit Entrepreneurship** - Join discussions and learn from fellow entrepreneurs on Reddit.

5. **Canva** - Create professional graphics and designs for social media and digital marketing.

6. **NKS Digital Media** – Website offers free resources across all digital marketing aspects

Appendix 3: Legal Considerations and Best Practices

In this appendix, we will cover the legal aspects and best practices essential for running a successful digital media business. Understanding and adhering to legal requirements is crucial for protecting your business, maintaining credibility, and avoiding potential legal issues.

Copyright and Intellectual Property

1. **Understanding Copyright Law:**

    o **Description:** Learn the basics of copyright law, including what can be copyrighted and how to protect your original content.

    o **Best Practices:** Always create original content or obtain proper licenses for using third-party materials. Consider registering your works with the appropriate copyright office.

2. **Fair Use:**

    o **Description:** Understand the concept of fair use and how it applies to your content.

    o **Best Practices:** Ensure your use of copyrighted material falls under fair use by considering factors such as purpose, nature, amount, and effect on the market.

3. **Trademark Protection:**

    o **Description:** Learn how to protect your brand name, logo, and other trademarks.

    o **Best Practices:** Conduct thorough searches before using a new brand name or logo to avoid infringing on existing trademarks. Register your trademarks with the appropriate government office.

Privacy and Data Protection

1. **Data Privacy Regulations (e.g., GDPR, CCPA):**

   o **Description:** Understand key data privacy laws that may affect your business.

   o **Best Practices:** Implement clear privacy policies, obtain user consent for data collection, and ensure data security measures are in place.

2. **User Data Management:**

   o **Description:** Learn how to responsibly collect, store, and manage user data.

   o **Best Practices:** Only collect necessary data, store it securely, and provide users with options to access, correct, or delete their information.

Advertising and Marketing Compliance

1. **ASA Guidelines:**

   o **Description:** Familiarise yourself with the ASA (Advertising Standards Authority) standards which regulate advertising in UK across all media, ensuring ads are legal, decent, honest, and truthful. Federal Trade Commission (FTC) guidelines on advertising and endorsements is the US equivalent.

   o **Best Practices:** Disclose any paid partnerships or sponsored content clearly and conspicuously. Avoid making false or misleading claims.

2. **Email Marketing Laws (e.g., PECR):**

   o **Description:** Learn the legal requirements for sending marketing emails.

   o **Best Practices:** Obtain explicit consent from recipients, provide a clear opt-out option, and include your business's physical address in all emails.

Contracts and Agreements

1. **Content Licensing Agreements:**

   o **Description:** Understand the importance of licensing agreements when using third-party content.

   o **Best Practices:** Ensure all content used in your digital media is properly licensed and that you have the necessary permissions in writing.

2. **Collaboration and Partnership Agreements:**

   o **Description:** Learn how to draft and negotiate agreements with collaborators and partners.

   o **Best Practices:** Clearly outline the terms, responsibilities, and compensation in any partnership agreements to avoid disputes.

Protecting Your Online Presence

1. **Website Terms of Service and Privacy Policy:**

   o **Description:** Create comprehensive terms of service and privacy policy for your website.

   o **Best Practices:** Regularly update these documents to reflect changes in your business practices and legal requirements.

2. **Cybersecurity Measures:**

  ○ **Description:** Implement cybersecurity best practices to protect your digital media assets.

  ○ **Best Practices:** Use strong passwords, enable two-factor authentication, regularly update software, and educate your team about phishing and other cyber threats.

By understanding these legal considerations and adhering to best practices, you can protect your digital media business, build trust with your audience, and operate within the bounds of the law.

Glossary Of Terms

Ad Revenue: Income generated from advertisements placed on digital media platforms, such as websites, YouTube channels, and podcasts. Advertisers pay content creators based on impressions, clicks, or other metrics.

Affiliate Marketing: A performance-based marketing strategy where content creators earn commissions by promoting products or services and driving sales through unique affiliate links.

Analytics: Tools and processes used to measure and analyse data related to the performance of digital content. Key metrics include website traffic, social media engagement, and conversion rates.

Automation Tools: Software that automates repetitive tasks in digital media management, such as scheduling posts, sending emails, and tracking analytics. Examples include Hootsuite, Buffer, and Mailchimp.

Branding: The process of creating a unique identity for a digital media presence, including name, logo, colour scheme, and overall aesthetic. Strong branding helps distinguish content and build audience recognition.

Content Calendar: A planning tool that outlines the schedule for creating and publishing digital media content. It helps maintain consistency and organise topics, formats, and posting dates.

Crowdfunding: A method of raising funds by soliciting small amounts of money from a large number of people, typically via online platforms like Kickstarter, Patreon, or GoFundMe.

Digital Marketing: The use of online channels to promote products, services, or content. Techniques include SEO, social media marketing, email marketing, and paid advertising.

E-commerce: The buying and selling of goods and services online. Digital media creators can use e-commerce platforms to sell products, merchandise, or digital downloads directly to consumers.

Evergreen Content: Content that remains relevant and valuable over time, as opposed to time-sensitive content. Evergreen content continues to attract traffic and engagement long after it is published.

Influencer: An individual with a significant online following who can influence their audience's opinions and purchasing decisions. Influencers often collaborate with brands for sponsored content.

Keywords: Words or phrases that describe the content of a web page or digital media. Keywords are used in SEO to improve a website's visibility in search engine results.

Monetisation: The process of generating revenue from digital media content through various methods such as ad revenue, affiliate marketing, sponsored content, merchandise sales, and subscription models.

Niche: A specific segment of the market or audience that a content creator focuses on. A well-defined niche helps attract a dedicated and engaged audience.

SEO (Search Engine Optimisation): Techniques used to improve the visibility of a website or content in search engine results pages. Effective SEO increases organic traffic and engagement.

Social Media Engagement: Interaction between digital media creators and their audience on social media platforms. Engagement includes likes, comments, shares, and direct messages.

Sponsored Content: Paid collaborations between content creators and brands, where the creator promotes the brand's products or services in their content. Sponsored content should be clearly disclosed to the audience.

Subscription Models: A revenue model where users pay a recurring fee for access to premium content, services, or membership benefits. Common in digital media, it provides a steady income stream.

Thumbnails: Small preview images that represent a video or other digital content. Engaging thumbnails attract viewers and improve click-through rates.

Traffic: The number of visitors to a website or viewers of digital content. Traffic can be organic (from search engines), direct (typing the URL), or referred (from other websites or social media).

Vlog (Video Blog): A type of blog where the content is presented in video format. Vloggers share experiences, tutorials, reviews, and other topics through video.

Web Hosting: A service that provides the technology and infrastructure needed to make a website accessible on the internet. Reliable hosting ensures that a website runs smoothly and is available to visitors.

YouTube Partner Program: A program that allows YouTube creators to monetise their channels through ad revenue, channel memberships, Super Chat, and other features once they meet certain eligibility criteria

About the Author: Nathan Shewring

Nathan Shewring has a rich background deeply rooted in advertising and marketing, having grown up within a family business specialising in these fields. This early exposure provided him with extensive knowledge and experience that have been pivotal throughout his career.

Nathan pursued higher education with dedication, earning an honours degree in Computing and Statistics. This academic achievement ignited his passion for technology, leading him to explore various facets of the field, including software programming and networking infrastructures. His technical expertise facilitated a natural progression into IT project and program delivery, an area in which he has amassed several professional qualifications.

Throughout his career, Nathan has been instrumental in building and developing websites for recruitment and project management firms. This experience paved the way for his transition into the finance sector, where he gained a solid understanding of financial markets and engaged in personal trading endeavours.

Currently, Nathan holds a senior role in a large multinational organisation, where he is responsible for delivering complex IT infrastructure programs. His commitment to continuous learning and professional development is evidenced by his recent certification in the building construction industry through the Royal Institution of Chartered Surveyors (RICS).

Beyond his professional achievements, Nathan is a dedicated sportsman. He devotes a significant portion of his time to managing his son's football team, demonstrating his leadership skills and commitment to fostering young talent.

Nathan Shewring's multifaceted career, from advertising to IT and finance, coupled with his active involvement in grass-root sports, showcases a blend of technical acumen, strategic insight, and community dedication.

Index

www.ingramcontent.com/pod-product-compliance
Lightning Source LLC
Chambersburg PA
CBHW071946210526
45479CB00002B/836